A Guide for Using

The Phantom Tollbooth

in the Classroom

Based on the novel written by Norton Juster

*This guide written by **Kathleen L. Bulloch***
Illustrated by Theresa M. Wright

Teacher Created Materials, Inc.
6421 Industry Way
Westminster, CA 92683
www.teachercreated.com

©*1994 Teacher Created Materials, Inc.*
Reprinted, 2004

Made in U.S.A.

ISBN 1-55734-431-0

Table of Contents

Introduction

A good book can touch our lives like a good friend. Within its pages are words and characters that can inspire us to achieve our highest ideals. We can turn to it for companionship, recreation, comfort, and guidance. It can also give us a cherished story to hold in our hearts forever.

In *Literature Units*, great care has been taken to select books that are sure to become good friends. Teachers who use this literature unit will find the following features to supplement their own valuable ideas.

- Sample Lesson Plans
- Pre-Reading Activities
- Biographical Sketch and Picture of Author
- A Book Summary
- Vocabulary Lists and Suggested Vocabulary Activities
- Chapters grouped for study with each section including:

    —*quizzes*
    —*hands-on projects*
    —*cooperative learning activities*
    —*cross-curriculum connections*
    —*extensions into the reader's own life*

- Post-Reading Activities
- Book Report Ideas
- Research Ideas
- Culminating Activity
- Three Different Options for Unit Tests
- Bibliography
- Answer Key

We are confident that this unit will be a valuable addition to your planning, and we hope that as you use our ideas, your students will increase the circle of "friends" that they can have in books!

Sample Lesson Plan

Each of the lessons suggested below can take from one to several days to complete.

Lesson 1

- Introduce and complete some or all of the pre-reading activities found on page 5.
- Read "About the Author" with your students. (page 6)
- Read the book summary with your students. (page 7)
- Introduce vocabulary list for Section 1. (page 8) Ask students to find all possible definitions for vocabulary words.

Lesson 2

- Read chapters 1 through 4. As you read, place the vocabulary words in the context of the story and discuss their meanings.
- Choose a vocabulary activity. (page 9)
- Make clay alphabet letters. (page 11)
- Plan a class trip. (page 12)
- Create a list of questions based on the map. (page 13)
- Begin "Reader's Response Journals". (page 14)
- Administer the Section 1 quiz. (page 10)
- Introduce vocabulary list for Section 2. (page 8) Ask students to find all possible definitions.

Lesson 3

- Read chapters 5 through 8. Place the vocabulary words in context and discuss their meanings.
- Choose a vocabulary activity. (page 9)
- Design a personal coat of arms. (page 16)
- Plan an alliteration lunch. (page 17)
- Research word origins. (page 18)
- Discuss dealing with fears. (page 19)
- Administer Section 2 quiz. (page 15)
- Introduce vocabulary list for Section 3. (page 8) Ask students to find all possible definitions.

Lesson 4

- Read chapters 9 through 12. Place vocabulary words in context and discuss their meanings.
- Choose a vocabulary activity. (page 9)
- Make a sound bender. (page 21)
- Perform a colorful experiment. (page 23)
- Play charades. (page 22)
- Chart and discuss different viewpoints. (page 24)
- Administer the Section 3 quiz. (page 20)

- Introduce vocabulary list for Section 4. (page 8) Ask students to find all possible meanings.

Lesson 5

- Read chapters 13 through 16. Place vocabulary words in context and discuss their meanings.
- Choose a vocabulary activity (page 9)
- Make a Mr. Dodecahedron. (page 26)
- Play a number game. (page 27)
- Complete journal entry for Digitopolis. (page 28)
- Discuss idioms. (page 29)
- Administer the Section 4 quiz. (page 25)
- Introduce vocabulary list for Section 5. (page 8) Ask students to find all possible meanings.

Lesson 6

- Read chapters 17 through 20. Place the vocabulary words in context and discuss their meanings.
- Choose a vocabulary activity. (page 9)
- Write a disappearing ink message. (page 31)
- Interview a friend. (page 32)
- Draw and color the demons from the Mountains of Ignorance. (page 33)
- Discuss qualities and characteristics of friendships. (page 34)
- Administer the Section 5 quiz. (page 30)

Lesson 7

- Discuss any questions your students may have about the story. (page 35)
- Assign book report and research projects. (pages 36-37)
- Begin work on Festival of Knowledge culminating activity. (pages 38-41)

Lesson 8

- Administer unit tests 1, 2, and/or 3. (pages 42, 43, 44)
- Discuss the test answers and responses.
- Discuss the students' opinions and enjoyment of the book.
- Provide a list of related reading for the students. (page 45)

Lesson 9 *(Optional)*

- Celebrate Festival of Knowledge culminating activity. (pages 38-41)

4

Before the Book

Before you begin reading The Phantom Tollbooth with your students, do some pre-reading activities to stimulate interest and enhance comprehension. Here are some activities that might work well in your class.

1. Predict what the story might be about by hearing the title.

2. Predict what the story might be about by looking at the cover illustration.

3. Answer these questions:

    Are you interested in:

    – stories about imaginary lands?
    – stories that make you laugh and think?
    – stories about unusual characters?
    – traveling to new places?
    – creating things to do when you are bored?

    Would you ever:

    – take a trip by yourself to a strange place?
    – move alone to a foreign country to live with people you have only met through letters?
    – risk your life to rescue a stranger?
    – risk your life to help a friend?

    Have you ever:

    – fantasized about an imaginary world?
    – planned a vacation trip?
    – had to act courageously in the face of danger?

4. Work in groups or as a class to create illustrated stories depicting an imaginary place.

About the Author

Norton Juster was born on June 2, 1929 in New York City.

Mr. Juster earned a Bachelor of Architecture degree in 1952 from the University of Pennsylvania and completed graduate studies at Liverpool University in England.

He worked for several years as an architect in Brooklyn, New York. He has also been an Assistant Professor of Design at Pratt Institute and Hampshire College. His military service included active duty from 1954-57 in the United States Naval Reserve, Chief Engineer Corps. On August 15, 1964, Mr. Juster married Jeanne Ray, a book designer.

In addition to *The Phantom Tollbooth* (Random House, 1961), this talented architect, teacher, and author wrote *The Dot and the Line* (Random House, 1963), *Alberic the Wise and Other Journeys* (Pantheon, 1965), and *Stark Naked* (Random House, 1970). His biography is included in the 1968 edition *The Who's Who of Children's Literature* (Schocken Books). An animated full-length feature of The Phantom Tollbooth was released by MGM in 1970 and is available on videocassette. In 1971 Norton Juster was the recipient of the George G. Stone Center for Children's Books Seventh Recognition of Merit.

The Phantom Tollbooth

by Norton Juster

(Alfred A. Knopf, Inc., 1989)

Milo, the hero in The Phantom Tollbooth, is a little boy with a big problem. He is bored. Milo isn't just bored sometimes; he is always bored. Nothing interests him, and he regards the process of seeking knowledge as a big waste of time. Then one day Milo discovers a large package in the corner of his bedroom. Inside it is a genuine turnpike tollbooth just waiting to be erected. When Milo drives his electrical car through the tollbooth gate, he finds himself in The Lands Beyond-enchanting home of creatures more strange than he could have ever imagined.

Milo meets a ticking watchdog named Tock, who travels with him to Dictionopolis, the city of words, located in the foothills of Confusion near the Sea of Knowledge. Here people buy and sell letters in the marketplace, words grow on trees in orchards, and people eat their own words. While in Dictionopolis, Milo and Tock are imprisoned with Faintly Macabre, the not-so-wicked Which. She tells Milo the history of the kingdom and describes how Princess Rhyme and Princess Reason have been banned from Wisdom and sent to live in the Castle in the Air.

Later, joined by Humbug, the two travel to Digitopolis, the city of numbers. The Ruler of Digitopolis, Mathemagician, gives them a tour of a cavern where numbers are mined and precious gemstones are simply discarded as worthless. Along the way, Milo has the rare opportunity to orchestrate a sunrise and meet interesting characters. Among the strange people he meets is Dr. Dischord who specializes in noises; Alec Bings who "stands" suspended in mid-air three feet from the ground and sees through things; and a faceless man who thinks the most important thing to do is a useless task.

Then Milo and his two companions courageously embark on a quest through the Mountains of Ignorance. With the black-hearted demons in pursuit, the three bring Rhyme and Reason once more to reign in Wisdom and restore peace between King Azaz, ruler of Dictionopolis, and Mathemagician, ruler of Digitopolis.

During Milo's incredible adventures, he learns that life isn't dull. It is rich with words and numbers, and full of exciting possibilities limited only by his imagination!

Vocabulary Lists

On this page are vocabulary lists which correspond to each sectional grouping of chapters, as outlined in the Table of Contents (page 2). Vocabulary activity ideas can be found on page 9 of this book. Because of the rich vocabulary experience offered in The Phantom Tollbooth, it is highly recommended that a significant amount of time be devoted to vocabulary and discussions about figurative language.

Section 1 *(Chapters 1-4)*

speculate	monotonous	disdain	reticence	infuriate
indignantly	tollbooth	precaution	lethargy	procrastinate
cartographer	ordinance	conciliatory	destination	flabbergast
unethical	dawdle	principality	balderdash	quagmire
surmise	loiter	presume	disrepute	proclamation
minstrels	misapprehension	tumult	bunting	palatinate

Section 2 *(Chapters 5-8)*

suspicious	brevity	wreaking	corrupts	havoc
miserly	macabre	barren	flickering	dank
domain	presumption	vaulted	prosperous	commendable
animosity	contemplating	provision	controversies	reconcile
arbitration	ominously	agitated	superfluous	conveyance
brougham	shandrydan	charabanc	signet	rigmarole
ragamuffin	indigestion	harrowing	chasms	crags

Section 3 *(Chapters 9-12)*

lure	promontory	magenta	contradict	chartreuse
inconvenient	illuminated	complicated	apothecary	cascade
deficiency	metropolis	exasperated	illusion	concocting
mirage	din	shaft	pandemonium	profusion
laudable	podium	disconsolate	gaunt	consensus
inquisitively	banished	constellations	interlude	pigment
crestfallen	spectrum	accurate	poised	dissonance

Section 4 *(Chapters 13-16)*

ominous	nuisance	console	vigorously	buffing
knickers	infinity	strenuous	caldron	billowy
savory	pungent	beret	logical	admonishing
famine	grimace	theatrical	accustomed	magnitude
stalactites	precise	honeycombed	distinction	daintily
complex	imaginary	convincingly	melancholy	intimidated
banished	pining	brandishing	furrow	interpret

Section 5 *(Chapters 17-20)*

indignantly	silhouettes	villainous	frock	ogre
ledger	punctuated	plunged	deliberation	murky
loathsome	precariously	destination	ovation	gnarled
plateau	compromise	lurch	invariably	calloused
bulbous	unkempt	grotesque	colossal	hideous
conspicuous	pathetic	gelatinous	proclamation	desperately
pavilions	assumption	desolate	lumbered	intruders

Vocabulary Activity Ideas

Each section contains several vocabulary words. You may wish to divide these words and assign them to small groups of students. The groups may define the words, find them in the context of the book, and present the information to the class to record in a vocabulary notebook.

You can help your students learn and retain the vocabulary in The Phantom Tollbooth by providing them with interesting vocabulary activities. Here are some ideas to try:

❑ Encourage students to make their own **Crossword or Wordsearch Puzzles** using the vocabulary words from the novel.

❑ Challenge your students to a **Vocabulary Bee.** This is similar to a spelling bee, but in addition to spelling each word correctly, the game participants must correctly define the words.

❑ Play **Vocabulary Concentration**. The goal of this game is to match vocabulary words with their definitions. Divide the class into groups of 2-5 students. Have students make two sets of cards the same size and color. On one set have them write the vocabulary words. On the second set have them write the definitions. All cards are mixed together and placed face down on a table. A player picks two cards. If the player matches the word with its definition, the player keeps the cards and takes another turn. It the cards don't match, they are returned to their places face down on the table, and another player takes a turn. Players must concentrate to remember the locations of words and definitions. The game continues until all matches have been made. This is an ideal activity for free exploration time.

❑ Have your students practice their writing skills by creating sentences and paragraphs in which multiple vocabulary words are used correctly. Ask them to share their **Vocabulary Sentences and Paragraphs** with the class.

❑ Challenge your students to use a specific vocabulary word from the story at least **10 Times in One Day!** They must keep a record of when, how, and why the word was used.

❑ As a group activity, have students work together to create an **Illustrated Dictionary** of vocabulary words.

❑ Play **20 Clues** with the entire class. In this game, one student selects a vocabulary word and gives clues about this word, one by one, until someone in the class guesses the word.

❑ Play **Vocabulary Charades**. In this game, vocabulary words are acted out.

You probably have many more ideas to add to this list. Try them. See if experiencing vocabulary on a personal level increases your students' vocabulary interest and retention!

Quiz Time!

1. On the back of this paper, list three major events of this section. Then complete the rest of the questions on this page.

2. How does Milo feel when the story begins?

   _____

3. Who are the Lethargarians?

   _____

4. Why was a dog that makes the sound "tickticktick" named Tock?

   _____

5. Name King Azaz's advisors.

   a) _____

   b) _____

   c) _____

   d) _____

   e) _____

6. What did Milo eat at the marketplace, and what was his reaction?

   _____

7. In one complete sentence, describe the Spelling Bee.

   _____

8. In one complete sentence, describe Humbug.

   _____

9. What did Milo learn from Tock

   _____

10. List three new concepts that Milo discovered from his experiences in this section.

   a) _____

   b) _____

   c) _____

Make Alphabet Letters

Milo found a variety of letters and words in the market place. There were fresh picked ifs, ands, and buts; nice ripe wheres and whens. Your students will be able to make their own alphabet letters with this easy chemical clay recipe. After the clay hardens, the letters can be painted and used as paperweights.

The following recipe makes a lump of clay about the size of a softball. Clay can be prepared by the teacher before class or by students during class with adult supervision.

Materials you will need:

- hot plate or portable camping stove
- ½ cup (125 mL) cornstarch
- 1 cup (250 mL) salt
- ¾ cup (175 mL) water
- heavy cooking pot
- pie tin or aluminum foil
- mixing spoon

Directions:

1. Mix salt and cornstarch in the cooking pot.

2. Slowly stir in the water. Keep stirring until the mixture is smooth.

3. Stirring continually, cook the mixture over low heat until it is stiff, like mashed potatoes. (This will take about 2 or 3 minutes.)

4. Spoon the mixture onto the pie tin or piece of aluminum foil. Let it cool for about 10 minutes.

5. When the mixture is cool enough to handle, press and knead it until it feels like clay (about 3-4 minutes).

Give each student a handful of clay so he or she can mold a letter or word.

Note: Pieces of clay must be moistened with water before they will adhere to each other. The clay dries to a stone-like finish and is very strong and durable. When the alphabet letter is dry, paint it with tempera paint. To store unused clay, wrap it in wax paper. It will keep for several days.

Beyond the Phantom Tollbooth

In the beginning of *The Phantom Tollbooth*, Milo was given a road map, a book of rules and regulations, and assorted coins for his journey. Have your students divide into groups. Their challenge is to plan a trip. In preparing their plans, students should note the following:

- destination (real or imaginary)
- length of trip
- mode of transportation
- what to pack in suitcase
- climate of destination
- currency used
- language spoken
- what sights they can expect to see

Have a spokesman for each group present the plans to the whole class. Students may choose to present the information as an advertisement for a travel agency.

As an extended activity, encourage students to create murals that depict their destinations. Use long strips of butcher paper attached to walls to create the mural backgrounds. Crayons, paints, markers, or colored paper cut outs can be used to add details to each mural.

Where in the World Is Milo?

Below is the road map Milo was given for his adventures through The Lands Beyond. Have students divide into pairs or groups and write six to eight questions concerning locations on the map.

Examples:

1. What direction do you travel to get to Digitopolis from the Valley of Sound?

2. If you are in the Doldrums, which is closer, the city of Dictionopolis or the Sea of Knowledge?

3. If you are in the Foothills of Confusion, what direction must you travel to get to the Island of Conclusions?

Extension Activity: Use an overhead projector to enlarge the map to the size of a bulletin board. Students can color in map sections and record Milo's progress as he journeys.

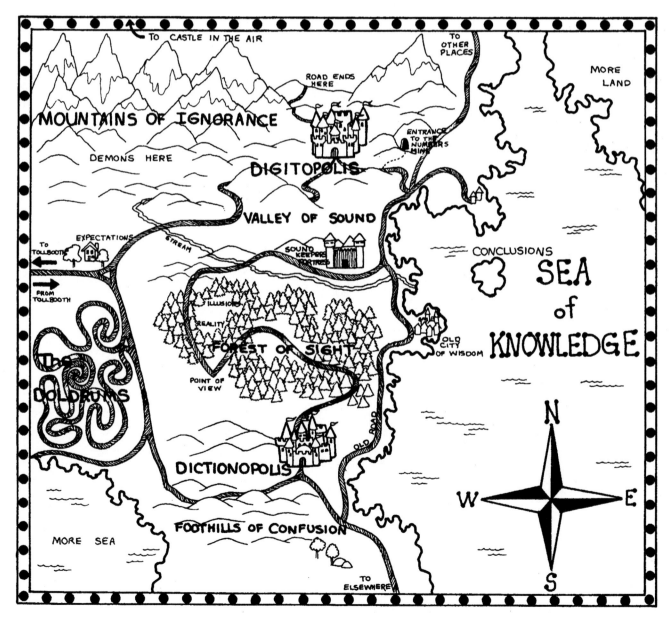

Reader's Response Journals

One reason avid readers are drawn to literature is what it does for them on a personal level. They are intrigued with how it triggers their imaginations, what it makes them ponder, and how it makes them see and shape themselves. To aid your students in experiencing this for themselves, incorporate Reader's Response Journals in your plans. In these individual journals, students can be encouraged to respond to the story in a number of ways. Here are a few ideas:

- Tell the students that the purpose of the journal is to record their thoughts, ideas, observations, and questions as they read the book.

- Provide students with, or ask them to suggest, topics from the story that may stimulate writing. Some examples of stimulus questions from chapters in Section 1 include:

    Milo traveled to a strange land. Have you, or would you, travel alone to an unfamiliar place?

    Milo met characters who looked strange and different. Have you ever found yourself in a place full of people you did not know? How did it make you feel?

- After reading each chapter, students may list one or more new things they learned.

- Ask the students to describe their favorite character or event in the story.

- Suggest to your students that they write a diary-type response to the reading by selecting a character and describing events from that character's point of view.

- Encourage students to bring journal ideas to life by using them to create plays, stories, songs, art displays, and/or debates.

- Students can respond to the story sequence by completing a format such as:

The Phantom Tollbooth		
Place	**Characters Met**	**Influence/Lesson Learned**

Allow students time to write in their journals daily. To evaluate the journals, you may wish to use the following guidelines.

Personal reflections will be read by the teacher, but no corrections or letter grades will be assigned. Credit is given for effort, and all students who sincerely try will be awarded credit. If a grade is desired for this type of entry, grade according to the number of journal entries completed, as required by the teacher. For example, if five journal entries were assigned and the student conscientiously completes all five, then he or she should receive an "A."

Non-judgmental teacher responses should be made as you read the journals to let students know that you are reading and enjoying journals, such as, "You've found an important point in that chapter!" or "You have made me feel as though I'm really there!"

Quiz Time!

1. On the back of this paper, list three major events in this section.

2. What is Spelling Bee's reaction to the wrecked word market stalls?

_____

_____

3. Who is Officer Shrift?

_____

4. What job did Faintly Macabre have years ago in Dictionopolis?

_____

_____

5. According to Faintly Macabre, how is the kingdom of Wisdom developed?

_____

_____

6. Why is it said by everyone that Rhyme and Reason answer all problems?

_____

_____

7. Where are Rhyme and Reason sent?

_____

8. What does King Azaz's palace look like?

_____

_____

9. What do Milo, Tock, and Humbug eat at the Royal Banquet? What do they have for dessert?

_____

_____

10. What does King Azaz give Milo for his journey? What instructions does he give to Milo?

_____

_____

My Personal Coat of Arms

One of the things Milo noticed in King Azaz's palace was the Royal Coat of Arms flanked by the flags of Dictionopolis.

Design your own personal coat of arms. Color and cut it out. Mount it on construction paper. Be prepared to explain the symbols on your coat of arms to classmates.

Note to teacher: Hang coats of arms in the classroom for a bulletin board display. Encourage students to design their own personal flags that may be used as a border for the bulletin board.

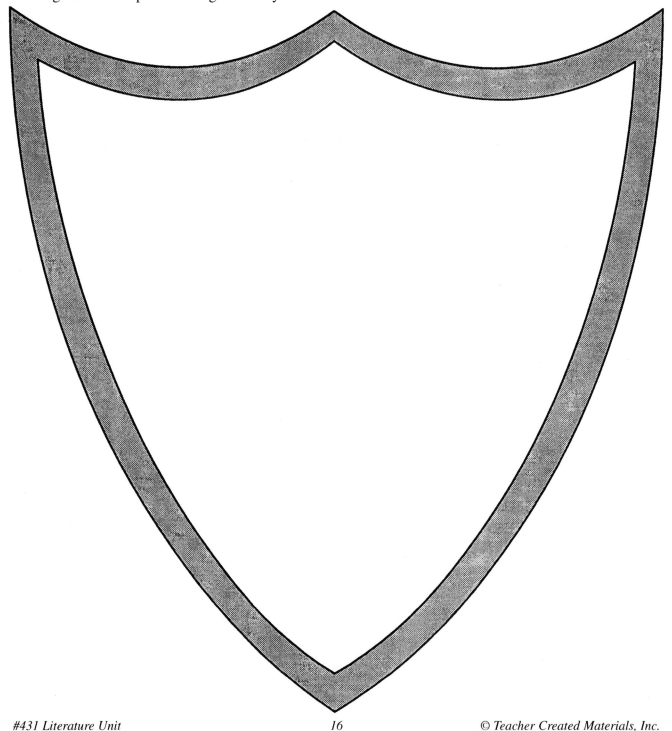

A Meal Fit for a King!

The Royal Banquet that Milo attended could have been much tastier if he had chosen his words more carefully! On the menu below, plan an alliteration lunch. (Alliteration is defined as the repeating of the same sound at the beginning of two or more words.) Include a main dish, side dish, dessert, and drink. Example for a B lunch: Boston baked beans, bologna on brown bread, baked bananas, and buttermilk. On the recipe card, write the directions for preparing one of the foods on your alliteration lunch menu.

Menu

_____   _____
        main dish   *dessert*

_____   _____
        side dish   *beverage*

Note to the teacher: On a teacher-designated picnic day, have each student bring one food beginning with a particular letter of the alphabet and have an alliteration picnic!

How Did We Get That Word?

King Azaz gave Milo a box of all the words that he knew. The study of word origins is fascinating. Use library reference books (see bibliography on page 45) to discover the origin of each of the words listed below. Add your own discoveries under "Others."

Foods

- hamburgers
- sandwich
- french fries
- ketchup

Animals

- hippopotamus
- poodle
- spider
- duck
- moose
- octopus

Household Items

- window
- pane
- attic
- kitchen
- wall
- roof

School Terms

- school
- book
- pens
- pencil
- pupils
- education

Science Terms

- telephone
- television
- automobile
- photograph
- astronaut
- aquarium

Others

-
-
-
-
-
-

Into the Unknown

Milo was about to embark on a dangerous journey in search of Princess Rhyme and Princess Reason. He would travel through miles of harrowing, hazardous countryside, unknown valleys, uncharted forests, and other perilous pitfalls.

Describe in detail a time when you had to overcome your fears to do something courageous, different, strange, or dangerous. Use these questions to plan your story description.

- How did you cope with your feelings of fear?

  _____

  _____

- How did you reassure yourself?

  _____

  _____

- Did you speak with someone about your feelings? If so, who was it, and how did he or she help you?

  _____

  _____

- Did you receive any recognition for your courageous deed?

  _____

  _____

- How did you feel after the ordeal?

  _____

  _____

- What advice would you give to someone who told you they were afraid?

  _____

  _____

Be prepared to share your writing with classmates.

Quiz Time!

1. On the back of this paper, list three major events in this section.

2. Who do Milo, Tock, and Humbug meet at Point of View?

_____

_____

3. In one or two complete sentences, describe what is unusual about Alec Bings.

_____

_____

4. Who lives in the small house in the forest? What is his secret?

_____

_____

5. Describe the differences between the cities of Reality and Illusion.

_____

_____

6. Who is Chroma the Great?

_____

7. In one or two complete sentences, describe the concert Milo attends in the forest.

_____

_____

8. What is Dr. Dischord's job?

_____

_____

9. In a complete sentence, describe Dynne.

_____

_____

10. Who lives in the Valley of Sound fortress? What is her job?

_____

Hear All About It!

Milo met Dr. Discord and the Soundkeeper, who both taught him interesting things about sounds. You can perform an experiment with sound. You can bend sound waves.

Materials you will need:

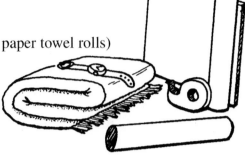

- cardboard (4" x 6"/10 x 15 cm strip)
- two cardboard tubes (both the same size, such as paper towel rolls)
- transparent tape
- towel
- watch (wind-up type)

Directions:

1. Place the paper tubes at right angles to each other as illustrated.

2. Place a folded towel at the free end of one of the tubes.

3. Lay the watch on the towel.

4. Place your ear close to the open end of the second towel tube.

5. Listen. Can you hear the watch ticking? No?

Now try it another way:

1. Place the piece of cardboard in a slanted position across the open space between the tubes as illustrated.

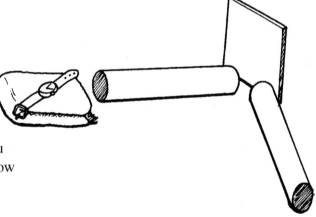

2. Place your ear close to the open end of the tube again. Listen. Do you hear the watch ticking now?

3. What happened? What has changed? Do you know why you can hear the watch ticking now but you couldn't before?

Scientific Principle:

Sound waves bounce off hard surfaces such as walls, floors, and ceilings. In this experiment, sound waves bounce around a corner. The sound waves made by the ticking watch traveled through the first tube. When the space was open, the sound waves simply went out the open end. But when you placed the cardboard between the tubes, it formed a bridge that directed the sound into the second tube and to your ear.

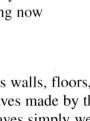

The Sounds of Silence

When Milo and his friends went to the Valley of Sound, they had the opportunity to discover what it was like to be in a place that was completely silent. They didn't like being in a place where there was no noise, and they soon discovered that it was very hard to communicate. How are you at communicating without words? Pantomime is the art of communicating a message without the use of voice or other sound. In pantomime, you use body language, facial expressions, and actions to convey your message.

Try playing charades. The basic idea is for someone to act out in pantomime a word or a series of words which an audience tries to guess. In a class, the game can be played with groups of 6-8 players. If your class is large, you can divide into four or five teams and have the winning team of each round play another winning group. One at a time the players of a given team act out their words while the other members of the team try to guess the charade. Each team performs the charade in the same way and is timed. After every team has had a turn, a timekeeper announces the team who finishes in the shortest amount of time as the winner. You can choose a non-player as the timekeeper. It doesn't matter how the charades are solved as long as the "mime" does not make any noise.

Once everyone understands pantomime, select a popular television show, movie, song, story, or poem to pantomime for the class.

It's a Colorful World!

Chroma demonstrated for Milo the incredible beauty in the colorful sunrise. Then Milo experimented and discovered that even colors need harmony. To celebrate Milo's interesting experiment with color, complete the project described below.

Materials you will need:

- coffee filter or paper toweling
- water-based markers in a variety of colors
- clear plastic cups with a small amount of water in each
- newspaper

Directions:

1. Using the water-based markers, draw symmetrical designs on coffee filters. Leave blank areas about the size of a quarter in the center of the filters.

2. Fold the coffee filters in half, and then in half a second time, forming cone shapes.

3. Submerge the tips of the coffee filters into the cups of water.

4. Observe what happens to the filter.

5. When the color has reached the edges of the filter, carefully remove filter from water, open it, and place on a newspaper to dry.

6. Try several colors and combinations of colors.

Scientific Principle:

Capillarity is the process by which water moves up the stem of a plant through hair-like tubes. Water is absorbed by the paper toweling or coffee filters by much the same process. When a water-based marker is used with one of these papers and then dipped in water, the ink will dissolve and spread out as the water moves up the paper. The inks that have been combined to form the different colors will separate at different speeds, producing a colorful design.

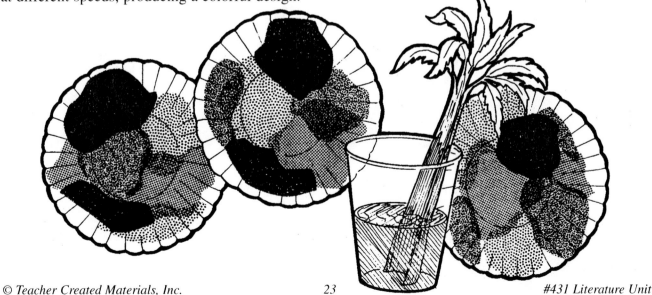

Point of View

Alec Bings taught Milo that everyone has his/her own point of view. "For instance, from here that looks like a bucket of water," he said, pointing to a bucket of water; "but from an ant's point of view it's a vast ocean, from an elephant's just a cool drink, and to a fish, of course, it's home. SO, you see, the way you see things depends a great deal on where you look at them from." To get a clearer picture of how important viewpoints are, complete the chart below. Read each item listed. Then respond to each from the appropriate viewpoint.

ITEM	Ant	Kitten	Mother	You
Favorite Lunch				
Sugar Cube				
Your Bed				
Goldfish				
Sneakers				
Yarn				

Quiz Time!

When Milo traveled to Digitopolis, he met Mr. Dodecahedron who often spoke in riddles. Below are some questions in the form of riddles. How many can you answer?

1. If numbers are mined in a cavern, what do they do with the broken pieces?

   _____

2. If you ate twenty-three bowls of subtraction stew, what would you get?

   _____

3. How many faces does Mr. Dodecahedron have?

   _____

4. If Mathemagician needs to be in two places at the same time, what does he do?

   _____

5. If you started saying it right now, when would you finish saying the smallest number possible?

   _____

6. Where do you keep the smallest number possible?

   _____

7. Why is Infinity a dreadfully poor place?

   _____

8. What is the only thing you can do easily in Digitopolis?

   _____

9. What did the Mathemagician have four million, eight hundred and twenty-seven thousand, six hundred and fifty-nine of?

   _____

10. In the cavern where numbers are mined, what did they do with diamonds, emeralds, rubies, and other precious gems?

    _____

11. Write your own math riddle.

    _____

The Man of Many Faces

You can make your own Mr. Dodecahedron with the pattern below. Cut along the solid lines. Use a black fine-tip marker to draw the many faces of Mr. Dodecahedron.

Fold inward along the dotted lines. Starting with flap A, glue the back of flap A to the edge marked A. Repeat by matching each letter of the alphabet (B matching B and so on). A dodecahedron gets its name from the fact that it is a solid shape with twelve equal sides.

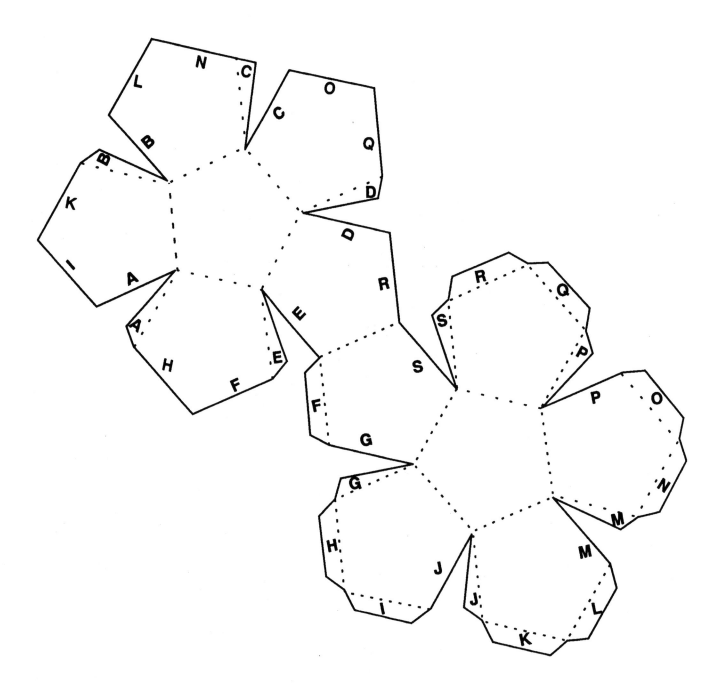

Become a Math Wizard

Mr. Dodecahedron and Mathemagician taught Milo that numbers can be friendly and fun. You and your friends can have fun with numbers too. The object of the game below is to get an appropriate person to autograph each space. When you find someone who fits the description found in the first space, have him/her autograph that space on your board and go on to the next space. You may not use the same person more than once on your game card. When all of the spaces are autographed, you win!

GO!	Someone whose hair is longer than thirteen inches (33 cm). ➡	Someone whose foot is about eight inches long (20 cm). ⬇
Someone who has traveled in an airplane more than 3,000 miles (5,000 km). ⬇	Someone who has three brothers and no sisters. ⬅	Someone who can multiply 12 x 23 in his/her head. ⬅
Someone who has a collection of more than 500 things. ➡	Someone who has lines in the palm of his/her hand that look like the digit three. ➡	Someone whose first, middle, and last names have a total of seventeen letters. ⬇
Someone who can count to one hundred by fives in less than five seconds. ⬇	Someone who knows someone living that is over one hundred years old. ⬅	Someone whose street address numbers total thirteen. ⬅
Someone who knows how many feet are in a mile or meters in a kilometer. ➡	Someone who has five pets. ➡	Someone whose first name has exactly seven letters. ⬇
End! Hooray for You!	Someone who can count by sevens to 98. ⬅	Someone who likes math better than reading or spelling. ⬅

Milo's Days with Digits

If Milo had kept a diary or journal of his adventures in Digitopolis, what would it have included? In complete sentences, write four journal entries describing things that Milo experienced. They might include: Milo's conversation with Dodecahedron, the Mathemagician Stew, the number mine, or his visit to the workshop.

Milo's Journal

Entry 1 _____
Date

Entry 1 _____
Date

Entry 1 _____
Date

Entry 1 _____
Date

Look Before You Leap!

In Chapter 13, "Unfortunate Conclusions," Milo and his companions suffer the consequences of literally "jumping to Conclusions."

> " '...you're on the Island of Conclusions. ...'
> 'But how did we get here?' asked Milo ...
> 'You jumped, of course,' explained Canby. 'That's the way most everyone gets here. It's really quite simple: every time you decide to do something without having a good reason, you jump to Conclusions whether you like it or not.' "

The phrase "jump to conclusions" is a type of figurative language called an idiom. Idioms are phrases or expressions which mean something different from what the words actually say.

Below is a list of commonly used idioms. You may be able to add others. Choose five or more, as directed by your teacher, from the list and write or draw a situation in which each idiom was taken literally instead of the way it was actually meant. Write the idiom below your picture or paragraph and then write what the idiom actually means.

- **Don't let the cat out of the bag.**
- **he's full of hot air.**
- **He's got a big head.**
- **Hittheroad.**
- **You're in the doghouse.**
- **Hold your horses.**
- **She's talking out of both sides of her mouth.**
- **It goes in one ear and out the other.**
- **Don't spill the beans.**
- **He has a green thumb.**
- **She's making a mountain out of a molehill.**
- **I'm all ears.**
- **I've got butterflies in my stomach.**
- **He has a heart of gold.**
- **Keep it under your hat.**
- **Put a lid on it.**

- **Let's put our heads together.**
- **It's a drop in the bucket.**
- **I'm all thumbs.**
- **He has two left feet.**
- **Keep a stiff upper lip.**
- **She'll have to pay through the nose.**
- **Mom and Dad bring home the bacon.**
- **The puppy was a real ball of fire.**
- **He's afraid of his own shadow.**
- **We'll work around the clock.**
- **It costs an arm and a leg.**
- **Stop beating around the bush.**
- **She caught his eye.**
- **He's down in the dumps.**
- **Drop me a line.**
- **Give me a ring.**
- **Others:**

Quiz Time!

1. On the back of this paper, list three major events of this section.

2. Describe the three tasks that Terrible Trivium asks Milo, Tock, and Humbug to do. What is the purpose of these tasks?

   a) _____

   b) _____

   c) _____

3. In a complete sentence, describe the Demon of Insincerity.

   _____

4. How do Milo and his friends escape from the Gelatinous Giant?

   _____

5. Who is curled up in front of the first spidery spiral stair?

   _____

6. List three of the questions the Senses Taker asks Milo and his friends.

   _____

   _____

   _____

7. How does the Senses Taker trick Milo, Tock, and Humbug?

   _____

   _____

8. Who lives in the Castle in the Air?

   _____

9. In reality, how long is Milo gone from his bedroom? What time does he return home?

   _____

10. What is the one important thing Milo learned on his quest to reach the Land of Infinity?

    _____

    _____

Now You See It, Now You Don't!

The Senses Taker tried to help Milo find what he was not looking for, but Milo was not fooled. Sometimes people see what isn't there or don't see what is there. You can write a message with ink that doesn't seem to be there.

Materials you will need:

- lemon Juice
- small dish or glass
- wooden toothpick
- electric bulb
- blank paper

Directions for the sender:

1. Put lemon juice into a small dish.

2. Dip the toothpick in lemon juice and write your message on paper. Short one or two-word messages work best because you may not be able to see what you are writing.

3. When lemon juice is dry, you are ready to send your message.

Directions for the receiver:

1. Hold the paper over a lighted electric bulb. Message should appear in less than a minute. Move the paper around until you can read all of the message.

Caution: Do not hold the paper too close to the bulb for a long period of time because it can ignite.

The Ledger of Life

Pretend that you are the Senses Taker and you need to complete your ledger.

Remember the many questions the Senses Taker asked Milo and his friends? Many of the questions were meaningless and the interview took so long that it annoyed Milo and his friends. See if you have more patience with these same questions. Interview a friend to complete the Official Senses Taker Questionnaire found below. Then let your partner interview you. Be prepared to share with the class an interesting thing you learned about your friend.

Official Senses Taker Questionnaire

Name _____

When were you born? _____

Where were you born?_____

Why were you born? _____

How old are you now?_____

How old were you when you were born? _____

How old will you be in a little while?_____

Mother's Name?_____

Father's Name? _____

Aunts' Names?_____

Uncles' Names? _____

Cousins' Names? _____

Where do you live? _____

How long have you lived there? _____

Which schools have you attended? _____

What are your hobbies?_____

What is your telephone number?_____

What is your shoe size? _____

What is your shirt size? _____

What is your collar size? _____

What is your hat size? _____

Name six people who can verify all the information given. _____

In the Dark

Milo, Tock, and Humbug met many demons in the Mountains of Ignorance. Draw a picture of each of these demons after you have read about them in *The Phantom Tollbooth*.

Demon of Insincerity	Threadbare excuse	Horrible Hopping Hindsight
First Demon of Compromise	**Second Demon of Compromise**	**Third Demon of Compromise**
Gorgons of Hate & Malice	**Overbearing Know-it-all**	**Gross Exaggeration**

Forever Friends

'Thank you for everything you've taught me, ' said Milo to everybody as a tear rolled down his cheek.
'And thank you for what you 've taught us, ' said the King

Milo met many characters who helped him throughout his journey. Think of five family members, friends, teachers, and/or classmates who have helped you gain valuable knowledge. Make a list of the people and describe what each has taught you.

Person	Lesson Learned

Extension Activities:

Write a thank-you letter to someone on your list recognizing the contribution he or she has made to your life. Tell that person how he or she has helped you. Remember to include all the parts of a letter: heading, return address, date, greeting, body, closing, and signature.

Pretend you are Milo. Write a thank-you letter to one or more of the characters who helped you.

In complete sentences, describe in detail how you settle disagreements and problems with family members or friends.

Be prepared to share your ideas with classmates.

Any Questions?

When you finished reading The Phantom Tollbooth, did you have any questions that were left unanswered? List your questions here:

_____

_____

_____

_____

_____

Work in groups, or by yourself, to prepare possible answers to some or all of the questions you have asked above and those listed below. When you have finished your predictions, share your ideas with the class.

1. What happened to Milo? Did he take another trip beyond the Phantom Tollbooth? Why?

2. Where did the Phantom Tollbooth appear after it left Milo's bedroom?

3. What did Milo tell his friends and family about his journey?

4. How did Milo's trip change his life forever?

5. What happened to King Azaz and Mathemagician? After Rhyme and Reason returned to Wisdom, how did the two brothers settle their differences about words vs. numbers?

6. What changes took place in the Lands Beyond after Milo left? In Dictionopolis? In Digitopolis?

7. What happened to Princess Reason and Princess Rhyme? What changes took place after they returned from the Castle in the Air?

8. What became of Tock and Humbug? Did Milo ever see them again?

9. What happened to the demons? Will they ever leave the Mountains of Ignorance?

10. What are some lessons the characters from The Land Beyond learned from Milo? How will Milo's visit change The Land Beyond for future visitors?

11. What will happen to Milo in the future? What kind of an adult do you think he will become?

Book Report Ideas

There are many ways to report on a book once it has been read. After you have finished *The Phantom Tollbooth*, choose a method of reporting on it that interests or appeals to you. It may be an idea of your own, a way your teacher suggests, or one of the suggestions mentioned below:

• The Eyes Have It

Do a visual report by making a model of a scene from the book, drawing or sculpting a likeness of one or more characters, or crafting an important symbol from the book.

• Time Capsule

Provide people in the future with reasons to read *The Phantom Tollbooth*. Inside a time-capsule-shaped design, neatly write your reasons why the book should be read. You may "bury" your time capsule after you share it with your class (perhaps for next year's class to find).

• Come to Life

Prepare a scene from the book for dramatization in a size-appropriate group, act it out, and relate the significance of the scene to the entire book. Costumes and props will add to the dramatization!

• Into the Future

Predict what might happen if the Phantom Tollbooth appears in some other child's bedroom. You may write it as a story in narrative form, a dramatic script, do a visual display, or perform a short skit.

• Guess Who or What

This report takes the form of "Twenty Questions." The reporter gives a series of clues about a character from the story in a general to specific order. After each clue, someone may try to guess the character. After all the clues, if the subject cannot be guessed, the reporter may tell the class. The reporter then does the same for an event in the book and then for an important object or symbol.

• A Character Comes to Life

Suppose one of the characters in *The Phantom Tollbooth* came to life and walked into your classroom? This report gives the character's point of view as he or she sees, hears, feels, and experiences the world in which you live.

• Sales Talk

This is an advertisement to sell *The Phantom Tollbooth* to one or more specific groups. You decide on the group to target and the sales pitch you will use. Include some kind of graphics in your presentation.

• Coming Attraction

The Phantom Tollbooth is about to be made into a movie. You have been chosen to design the promotional poster. Include the title, author of the book, listing of main characters and contemporary actors who will play them. Include a drawing from a scene in the book, and a paragraph synopsis of the story that will make audiences want to see the movie.

• Literature Interview

This report is done in pairs. One student will pretend to be a character in a story and steep himself completely in that character's persona. The other student will play the role of a radio or television interviewer, trying to provide the audience with insights into the character's personality and life that the audience most wants to know. It is the responsibility of the partners to create meaningful questions and appropriate answers.

• Dust Cover Jacket

Design a dust cover jacket for the novel by including the title, author, and an important scene, image, or character on the cover, a book summary on the inside flaps, a teaser (hint at the plot that will make people want to read the book) as well as quotable recommendations for the book (e.g. "the L.A. Times calls it the best fantasy novel ever") on the back.

Research Ideas

Describe three things you read in *The Phantom Tollbooth* you would like to learn more about:

1. _____

2. _____

3. _____

As you read *The Phantom Tollbooth*, you encountered many figures of speech, imaginary characters and places, ways of coping, and new attitudes about learning. To increase your understanding of the characters and events of the book, as well as to more fully recognize Norton Juster's craft as a writer, research to find out more about these people, places, and things.

Work in groups to research one or more of the areas you named above, or areas that are listed below. Share your findings with the rest of the class in any appropriate form of presentation.

- word origins
- history of English language
- invention of writing
- invention of alphabet
- history of tollbooths
- invention of last names
- *Canterbury Tales*
- Geoffrey Chaucer
- William Shakespeare
- Charles Dickens
- Sumerians/picture writing
- cuneiform tablet writing
- Henry Rawlinson
- *Gilgamesh*
- Hieroglyphics
- Semites/Alphabet
- Phoenician alphabet
- Greek alphabet
- Roman alphabet
- Flag alphabet
- finger spelling/Sign Language
- Louis Braille
- Braille
- poets
- authors
- reporters
- editors
- newscasters
- copywriters
- *Wizard of Oz*

- *Alice in Wonderland*
- heraldry
- Bible transcribers
- proverbs
- idioms
- negotiations
- antonyms
- homonyms
- synonyms
- verbs
- nouns
- adjectives
- adverbs
- translators
- linguistics
- speech/language
- pathologists
- audiologists
- lexicographers
- etymologists
- rebus
- invention of telegraph
- Marconi
- Alexander Graham Bell
- invention of telephone
- Morse Code
- time travel
- *Gulliver's Travels*
- Jules Verne

Festival of Knowledge

Celebrate the completion of reading The Phantom Tollbooth, as well as the knowledge you have gained, with a Festival of Knowledge in honor of the occasion. (You may choose to incorporate the festival with your school's Open House event.) Small groups may be organized to assist with the planning. The Brainstorming Sheet on page 40 may be used. Here are some ideas for projects, displays, and events for your Festival of Knowledge:

Projects and Displays

Designate areas in the classroom to be Dictionopolis, Digitopolis, City of Wisdom, etc. In each area display reading, math, or book reports. Encourage parents to tour through the "Phantom Classroom Lands!"

- Design a Tollbooth around the classroom door entrance. (See pattern idea on page 39.)
- Display pictures of characters from the book.
- Make letter-and number-shaped sugar cookies for refreshments.
- Create bulletin board and displays for students' work and projects done in this literature unit. (This includes projects on pages: 11, 16, 23, 31, 33).
- Display classroom diaries and research work.
- Let students design a Phantom Tollbooth board game.
- Have students make a wall mural of the map of The Lands Beyond. (See pattern on page 13.)
- Take photographs at the Festival of Knowledge. Make a scrapbook, including sample projects.
- Make marketplace booths to display student work, sell alphabet-shaped cookies, and alphabet posters, etc. Empty appliance boxes work well.

Events

- Have a spelling bee.
- Perform skits.
- Host a royal banquet (refreshments).
- Make banners.
- Write songs.
- Recite epic poems.
- Give speeches.
- Conduct math tournaments.
- Hold a reading tournament.
- Present scrolls of wisdom.
- Challenge student teams to find verbs, idioms, etc. in the book.
- Read portions of the book aloud. Each time a student hears an idiom, he/she claps hands.

Festival of Knowledge *(cont.)*

Use this page to brainstorm ideas for the Festival of Knowledge celebration.

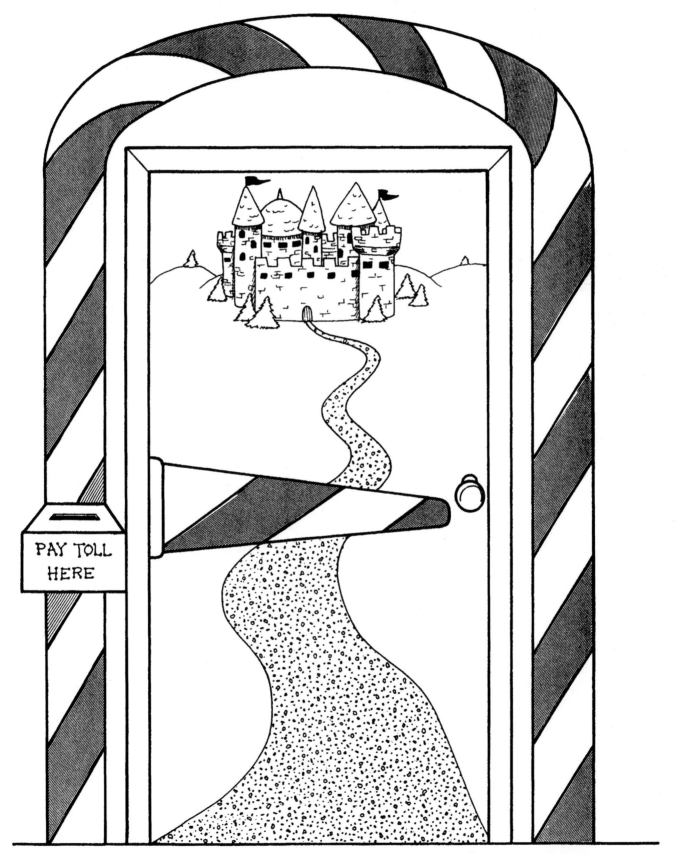

Brainstorming Sheet

Use this page to brainstorm ideas for the Festival of Knowledge celebration.

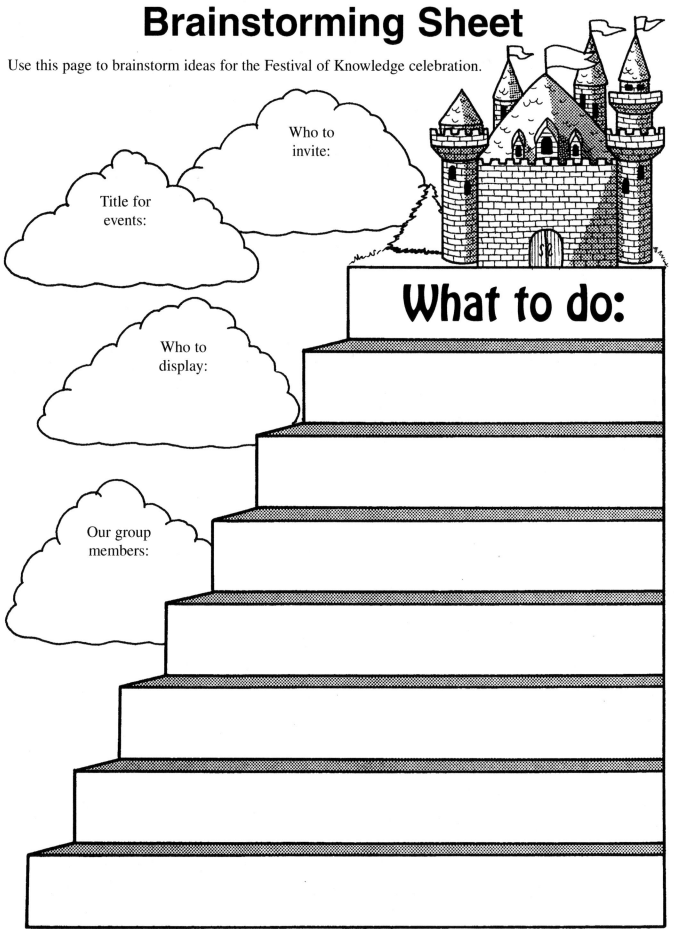

Who to
invite:

Title for
events:

Who to
display:

Our group
members:

What to do:

In Honor of Knowledge Award

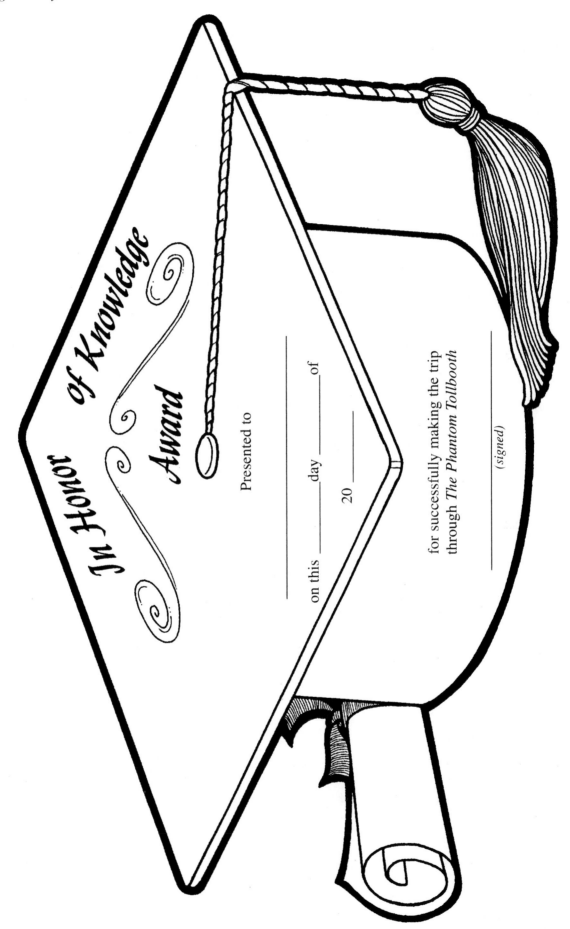

In Honor
of Knowledge
Award

Presented to

on this _____ day _____ of

20 _____

for successfully making the trip
through *The Phantom Tollbooth*

_____
(signed)

Objective Test and Essay

Matching: Match the names of the characters with their descriptions.

1._____ Short Shrift   A. disagreeable beetle

2._____ King Azaz   B. huge bumble bee who helps Milo spell

3._____ Faintly Macabre   C. ruler of Digitopolis

4._____ Mr. Dodecahedron   D. boy with a different point of view

5._____ Alec Bings   E. a 2 feet by 4 feet policeman

6._____ Tock   F. creature with 12 faces

7._____ Mathemagician   G. a not-so-wicked Which

8._____ Dr. Discord   H. another name for Watchdog

9._____ Humbug   I. the keeper of loud noises

10._____ Spelling Bee   J. king of letters in Dictionopolis

True or False: Write true or false next to each statement below.

1._____ Milo finds the Phantom Tollbooth in his backyard.

2._____ The first character Milo meets is the Whether Man.

3._____ Milo stops at the Market Place for numbers.

4._____ The Soundkeeper catalogues unpleasant noises.

5._____ The Mathemagician gives Milo a magic staff in the shape of a pencil.

Short Answers: Provide a short answer for each of these questions.

1. Who accompanied Milo on his journey?

2. What did the people eat at the Dictionopolis' Royal Banquet?

3. What did Mr. Chroma do at the beginning and end of each day?

4. What happened to the precious gemstones dug from the numbers mine?

5. Who tried to stop Milo in his quest by showing him a circus?

Essay: Answer these questions on the back of the paper.

1. Describe how Milo's outlook changed by the end of his journey.

2. Explain why Princess Rhyme and Princess Reason had to return to the Kingdom of Wisdom.

Response

Explain the meaning of each quote taken from The Phantom Tollbooth

Chapter 1:   *'Results are not guaranteed, but if not perfectly satisfied, your wasted time will be refunded.'*

Chapter 2:   *'Expect everything, I always say, and the unexpected never happens.'*

Chapter 3:   *'words [are] so confusing only when you use a lot to say a little . . .'*

Chapter 4:   *'Most people are just too lazy to make their own words,' ..., 'but it's much more fun.'*

Chapter 5:   *'always remember that while it is wrong to use too few [words], it is often far worse to use too many.'*

Chapter 6:   *'Words and numbers are of equal value, for, in the cloak of knowledge, one is warp and the other woof'*

Chapter 7:   *'I didn't know that I was going to have to eat my words, ' objected Milo.*

Chapter 8:   *'Things which are equally bad are also equally good. Try to look on the bright side of things.*

Chapter 9:   *'So, you see, the way you see things depends a great deal on where you look at them from.'*

Chapter 10:   *'the important reason for going from one place to another is to see what's in between...'*

Chapter 11:   *'I only treat illnesses that don't exist: that way, if I can't cure them, no harm done just one of the precautions of the trade.'*

Chapter 12:   *'It doesn't make me happy to hold back the sounds,...for if we listen to them carefully they can sometimes tell us things far better than words.'*

Chapter 13:   *'...every time you decide something without having a good reason, you jump to Conclusions whether you like it or not.'*

Chapter 14:   *'as long as the answer is right, who cares if the question is wrong?'*

Chapter 15:   *'The more you want, the less you get, and the less you get, the more you have. Simple arithmetic, that's all.'*

Chapter 16:   *'Then each of you agrees that he will disagree with whatever each of you agrees with,' said Milo triumphantly, 'and if you both disagree with the same thing, then aren't you really in agreement?'*

Chapter 17:   *'there's always something to do to keep you from what you really should be doing...,'*

Chapter 18:   *'As long as you have the sound of laughter,...I cannot take your sense of humor—and with it, you've nothing to fear from me.'*

Chapter 19:   *'so many things are possible just as long as you don't know they're impossible.'*

Choose appropriate number of quotes for students to respond.

Conversations

Work in size-appropriate groups to write or perform conversations that might have occurred in each situation:

- Milo and Tock talk about why Milo is bored. *(2 people)*

- Milo explains to his parents how he built the Tollbooth. *(3 people)*

- Whether Man describes the land of Expectations to Milo. *(2 people)*

- Tock explains the Doldrums to Milo. *(2 people)*

- The King's advisors invite Milo to the Market Place. *(6 people)*

- A Word Market seller deals with Milo, Tock, and Humbug. *(4 people)*

- Faintly Macabre tells the story of the land of Null to Tock, Milo, and Humbug. *(4 people)*

- Princess Rhyme and Princess Reason solve a dispute in the land of Wisdom between King Azaz and Mathemagician. *(4 people)*

- King Azaz and guests hold a conversation at the Royal Banquet. *(6 people)*

- Milo, Tock, and Humbug plan their trip to Castle in the Air. *(3 people)*

- Alec Bings describes Milo and friends to his family. *(4-6 people)*

- Milo interviews a resident of Illusion. *(2 people)*

- Dr. Discord works with Assistant Dynne in the Laboratory. *(2 people)*

- Soundkeeper explains the file system to Milo and friends. *(4 people).*

- Threadbare Excuse, Gross Exaggeration, and Overbearing Know-It-All plan to capture Milo on the Mountains of Ignorance. *(3-4 people)*

- Milo explains his journey to his younger brother or sister. *(2-3 people)*

Bibliography of Related Reading

Fantasy

Aiken, Joan. *The Last Slice of Rainbow and Other Stories.* (Harper, 1987)

Aiken, Joan. *Up the Chimney Down and Other Stories.* (Harper, 1985)

Babbitt, Natalie. *The Search for Delicious.* (Farrar, 1969) and others by this author

Banks, Lynne Reid. *The Indian in the Cupboard.* (Doubleday, 1981) and others by this author

Barrie, J. M. *Peter Pan.* (Henry Holt, 1987) in many editions

Baum, L. Frank. *The Wizard of Oz* (Henry Holt, 1982) and others in the series

Burnett, Frances Hodgson. *The Secret Garden.* (Dell, 1962) in many editions and film

Carroll, Lewis. *Alice's Adventures in Wonderland.* (Knopf, 1988) in many editions and sequels

Chew, Ruth. *Mostly Magic.* (Scholastic, 1982) and others by this author—easy-to-read

Dahl, Roald. *Charlie and the Chocolate Factory.* (Bantam, 1964) and others by this author

Fleming, Ian. *Chitty Chitty, Bang Bang.* (Amereon, 1964)

Kay, Alexander. *The Forgotten Door.* (Scholastic, 1986) and others by this author

L'Engle, Madeleine. *A Wrinkle in Time.* (Dell, 1962) and others by this author

Lewis, C.S. *The Lion, the Witch, and the Wardrobe.* (Macmillan, 1950) and others in the Narnia series

Lloyd, Alexander. *The Book of Three.* (Henry Holt, 1964) and others by this author

Norton, Mary. *The Borrowers.* (Harcourt, 1953) and others in the series

O'Brien, Robert C. *Mrs. Frisby and the Rats of NIMH.* (Macmillan, 1971)

Saint-Esuprey, Antoine de. *The Little Prince.* (Harcourt, 1943)

Stolz, Mary. *Cat in the Mirror.* (Dell, 1975)

Tolkien, John R. *The Hobbit.* (Houghton, 1984)

Words

Carver, Craig M. *A History of English in Its Own Words.* (HarperCollins, 1991)

Espy, Willard, R. *A Children's Almanac of Words at Play.* (Crown, 1982)

Kay, Cathryn Berger. *Word Works: Why the Alphabet Is a Kid's Best Friend.* (Little, 1985)

Merriam-Webster, *The New Book of Word Histories.* (Webster, 1981)

Sarnoff, Jane. *Words: A Book about the Origins of Everyday Words and Phrases.* (Macmillan, 1981)

Steckler, Arthur. *One Hundred and One Words and How They Began.* (Doubleday, 1979)

Tuban, Marion. *The Dove Dove: Funny Homograph Riddles.* (Ticknor, 1988) and others by this author and books about words

Numbers

Anno, Mitsumasa. *Anno's Mysteries Multiplying Jar.* (Putnam, 1983)

Burns, Marilyn. *Math for Smarty Pants.* (Little, 1982)

Fisher, Leonard Everett. *Number Art: Thirteen 123's from Around the World.* (Macmillan, 1982)

Schwartz, David M. *If You Made a Million.* (Lothrop, 1989)

Sitomer, Mindel. *How Did Numbers Begin?* (Harper, 1972)

Answer Key

Page 10

1. Accept appropriate responses.
2. He was bored and had nothing to do.
3. They are the creatures who live in the Doldrums.
4. When his brother was born, they named him Tick; he made the sound "tocktocktock." So when Tock was born, they thought he would make the same sound and they called him Tock. But then he made the sound, tickticktick. Both brothers were forever burdened with the wrong names.
5. a. Duke of Definition
   b. Minister of Meaning
   c. Earl of Essence
   d. Count of Connotation
   e. Undersecretary of Understanding
6. Milo eats the letter "A," and discovers that it is quite tasty and delicious.
7. Spelling Bee is a huge bumble bee that spells most every word he speaks.
8. Humbug is an unpleasant, negative beetle who can argue either side of any issue.
9. Milo learned the importance of time.
10. Answers will vary:

Expectations is the place you must always go before you get to where you're going.

When you don't pay attention, you may wake up to find yourself in the Doldrums where nothing ever happens and nothing ever changes and no one is allowed to think. Time is not something you should kill at or even waste.

Thinking is the only way out of the Doldrums.

You cannot get into the marketplace without a reason or at least an excuse.

Page 15

1. Accept appropriate responses.
2. He flew off in a huff.
3. He is a policeman in Dictionopolis.
4. She was in charge of choosing words for all occasions.
5. By a young Prince looking for the future.
6. They were able to settle all controversies fairly and reasonably.
7. They were banished to the Castle in the Air.
8. The palace looks like an enormous book.
9. They ate their own words. For dessert they ate half-baked ideas.
10. He gave him a small, heavy box the size of a schoolbook containing all the words the King knew. He instructed Milo to use the words to ask all the questions which have never been asked and to answer all the questions which have never been answered. Milo was to use them well and in the right places.

Answer Key *(cont.)*

Page 18

FOOD: *hamburgers*: Hamburger, Germany; *sandwiches*: named after Earl of Sandwich who invented it; french fries: potatoes in long strips called Frenching, then fried; *ketchup*: Chinese word ke-tsiap meaning taste.

ANIMALS: *hippopotamus*: river horse in Greek; *poodle*: German word pudelhund-dog that splashed water; *spider*: Old English spithre meaning spinner; *duck*: Old English duce meaning river; *moose*: Indian word meaning he strips off bark; *octopus*: okto pous meaning eight feet in Greek.

HOUSEHOLD: *window*: Viking word meaning wind eye; *pane*: English word panngr meaning piece of cloth; *attic*: Greek attikos of Athens meaning truly beautiful; *kitchen*: Latin coquina meaning a cooking place; *wall*: Roman word vallum meaning wall of posts; *roof*: Old English hrof meaning cover.

SCHOOL: *school*: Greek schole meaning spare time; *book*: Old English boc means inner bark of beech tree; pen: Latin word penna means feather; *pencil*: Latin word penicillus means brush or little tail; **pupils**: Latin pupillae means little dolls.

INVENTED: *telephone*: Greek tele means far and phone means sound; *television*: Greek for far sight; *automobile*: Greek for self moving; *photograph*: Greek for drawing light; *astronaut*: Greek for star sailor; *aquarium*: Latin for aquarius or water

Page 20

1. Accept appropriate responses.
2. They met Alec Bings.
3. Alec Bings grew down instead of up. He "stood" three feet off the ground. He could see through things.
4. The thinnest, fattest, tallest, shortest man. He was one and the same person.
5. One is real and the other is imaginary. Some people see what isn't there, while others cannot see what is there.
6. Chroma the Great was the conductor of colors.
7. He witnessed Chroma the Great orchestrating the sunset. As the orchestra played, the colors appeared.
8. He specialized in all kinds of noises.
9. Dynne was a thick bluish smog with bright yellow eyes and a large frowning mouth.
10. The Soundkeeper. She catalogued and filed sounds used to invent sounds.

Page 25

1. Make fractions.
2. You would get hungrier.
3. Twelve.
4. He simply multiplies.
5. You would finish saying the number before you began saying it.
6. You keep the smallest number possible in a box that's so small you can't see it, that's kept in a drawer that's so small you can't see it, in a dresser that's so small you can't see it, in a house that's so small you can't see it, on a street that's so small you can't see it, in a world that's so small you can't see it.
7. Infinity is dreadfully poor because they cannot make ends meet there.
8. The only thing you can do easily in Digitopolis is be wrong.
9. Mathemagician had that many hairs on his head.
10. They threw the gemstones away.

Answer Key *(cont)*

Page 30

1. Accept appropriate responses.

2. Move one pile from one place to another with tweezers. Empty well with eyedropper. Dig hole with needle. To waste time with worthless jobs.

3. He was a long-nosed, green-eyed, curly-haired, wide-mouthed, broad-shouldered, thick-necked, round-bodied, short-armed and bowlegged, big foot monster. In reality, however, he was just a small furry creature.

4. Milo showed him his box of ideas, and the giant got frightened and told them to leave.

5. The Senses Taker.

6. Accept appropriate answers.

7. He showed them imaginary sights, sounds, and smells.

8. Princess Rhyme and Princess Reason.

9. One hour. six p.m.

10. It was impossible to complete the journey.

Page 35

Answers will vary.

Page 42

Matching: 1. E   2. J   3. G   4. F   5. D   6. H   7. C   8. I   9. A   10. B

True or False: 1. False   2. True   3. False   4. False   5. True

Short Answers:

1. Tock, Humbug

2. They ate their own words.

3. He led the orchestra that played the sunrise and sunset.

4. They were dug up and thrown away.

5. Senses Taker

Essay: Answers will vary. Accept well-supported and reasonable responses.

Page 44

Perform conversations in class. Ask students to respond to the conversations in several different ways, such as: Are the conversations realistic? Is the vocabulary the characters used true to the character? etc.